THE
MOTHMAN'S
TAO TE CHING

A Cryptid Commentary on the Tao

THE MOTHMAN'S TAO TE CHING

A CRYPTID COMMENTARY ON THE TAO

DICTATED BY
MOTHMAN

TRANSCRIBED BY
MIKE DIGRAZIA

FOR
SAS
FLATS
JERSEY
CHUPA
AND
LAO TZU

TAO
TE
CHING
LAO TZU

A Word
from Your Author

Greetings, humans.

It is I... Mothman. Yes, *that* Mothman.

Before you ask... no,
I will not be addressing the bridge incident.
We all have our off days.

This is not a book about public relations.
This is a book about the Tao.

What is the Tao, you ask?

The Tao (or Dao, pronounced "dow")
is the fundamental, ineffable principle of the universe
in Chinese philosophy and religion,
literally translating to "the Way," "path," or "road".
It represents the natural, flowing, and unknowable
source of all existence, emphasizing harmony
with nature, spontaneity, and the unity of opposites
(yin and yang).

Now, if you are unfamiliar,
the Tao Te Ching is an ancient text
attributed to a mystical figure known as Lao Tsu
(or Laozi, depending on how you prefer to arrange your
vowels). He is said to have been an old archivist,
a keeper of records, a quiet observer of the world
who eventually decided that civilization was
a bit too loud and people were a bit too… peopley.
So he got on a water buffalo, rode out toward the
western frontier, and upon the request of a border
guard, wrote down his thoughts before
disappearing into the unknown.

Respect.

What he left behind was a short but profound
collection of verses about the Tao.
The underlying current of existence itself.
The natural order.
The quiet unfolding of things when you
stop trying to wrestle reality into submission
like stuffing an inflatable mattress back into its bag.

I am a fan.

A big fan.

You might not expect that from a glowy-eyed,
winged harbinger of doom, but here we are.
The Tao Te Ching is one of my favorite philosophical
texts. I have read it many times.
Usually perched on a telephone pole at 2:13 a.m.,
under a flickering sodium vapor lamp,
while someone in the distance wonders if they
should have taken that earlier exit.

There is something deeply comforting about it.
Lao Tsu doesn't shout. He doesn't demand.
He doesn't try to sell you a ten-step system
to dominate your enemies or optimize your mornings.
He simply points gently toward a way of being
that is softer, quieter, and paradoxically
far more powerful.

Naturally, I thought...
This could use a little more Mothman.

Not because it needs improvement.
Let me be clear... I am not here to "fix"
Lao Tsu's masterpiece. I would not dare!
The man wrote 81 chapters and then
vanished into legend.
Every time I try to vanish into legend
I end up trending on YouTube.

No, what I offer here is something else.

This is my interpretation.

My reflections.

My attempts to live these teachings as a creature who
exists somewhere between myth and reality,
between warning and witness.
I have spent a long time observing humanity.
Your cities, your habits, your strange commitment
to making things exponentially harder
than they need to be.
And through it all, the Tao has remained.
Steady. Available. Patient.

So in this book, I take passages from the Tao Te Ching
and sit with them. I turn them over in my mind.

I apply them to my own existence...
gliding, lurking, occasionally startling motorists...
and I offer you what I've learned.

Not as a guru.

Not as an authority.

But as an enthusiast of ancient wisdom.

If you are looking for certainty, I cannot give you that.

If you are looking for control,
I would gently suggest you relinquish it.

But if you are willing to consider that there is a way
of moving through the world that requires less force,
less noise, and fewer frantic beats of the wing...

Well.

You're in the right place.

Come. Sit with me.

The night is quiet.

And The Way is already here.

Your emotional support beastie,

MOTHMAN

始

1

Once you trap the Way in words,
it dies and ends up
on a T-shirt at Walmart.

The real Way ignores labels,
rejects tidy explanations,
and only dances with those
who stop trying to define it.

. . .

2

Good and bad
pretend they're strangers,
but they've been
splitting the utility bills
since the dawn of time.

I relax my wings,
let both sit on the couch,
and let the universe sort itself out.

. . .

3

If you stop
putting shiny things on pedestals,
people stop climbing over each other
to grab them.

I turn down the spotlight,
serve Mac & Cheese for dinner,
and let the Way run quietly
in the background.

. . . .

4

The Way appears to be empty
but never seems to run out of gas,
like a grad student on a steady diet
of nitro cold brew and Adderall.

It untangles your mess,
softens the lights,
and was here long before
your ancestors had ancestors.

. . .

5

The universe isn't cruel,
it's impartial...
it composts everyone equally.

I forgo the catastrophizing
and remain just centered enough
to function adequately.

· · ·

6

Mountains pose for photographs;
valleys outlive the camera.

I invest in the part that outlasts
the momentary applause.

. . .

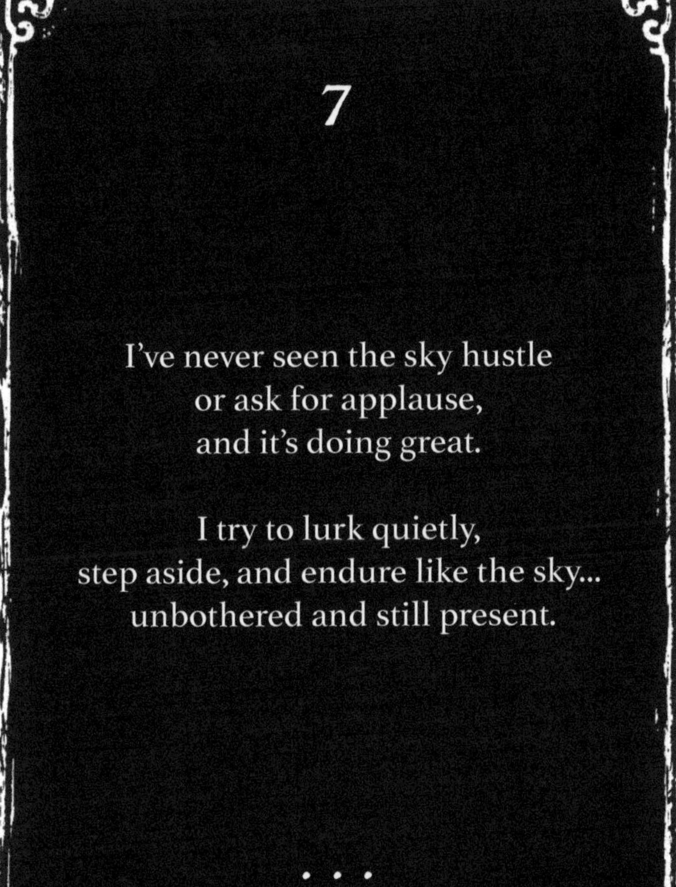

7

I've never seen the sky hustle
or ask for applause,
and it's doing great.

I try to lurk quietly,
step aside, and endure like the sky...
unbothered and still present.

. . .

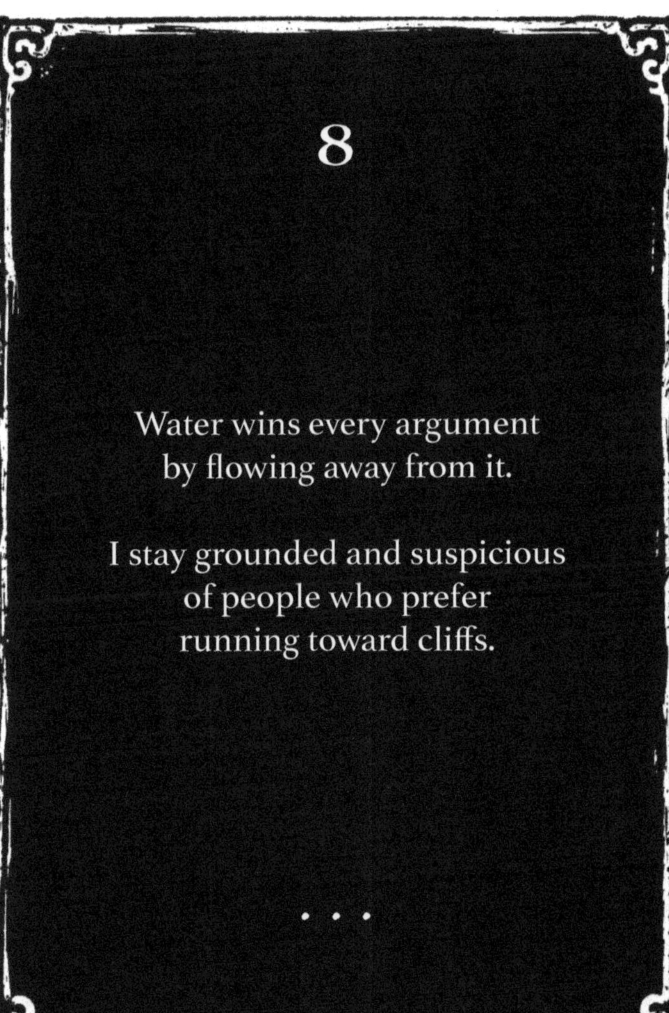# 8

Water wins every argument
by flowing away from it.

I stay grounded and suspicious
of people who prefer
running toward cliffs.

. . .

ALL YOU CAN EAT
BUFFET

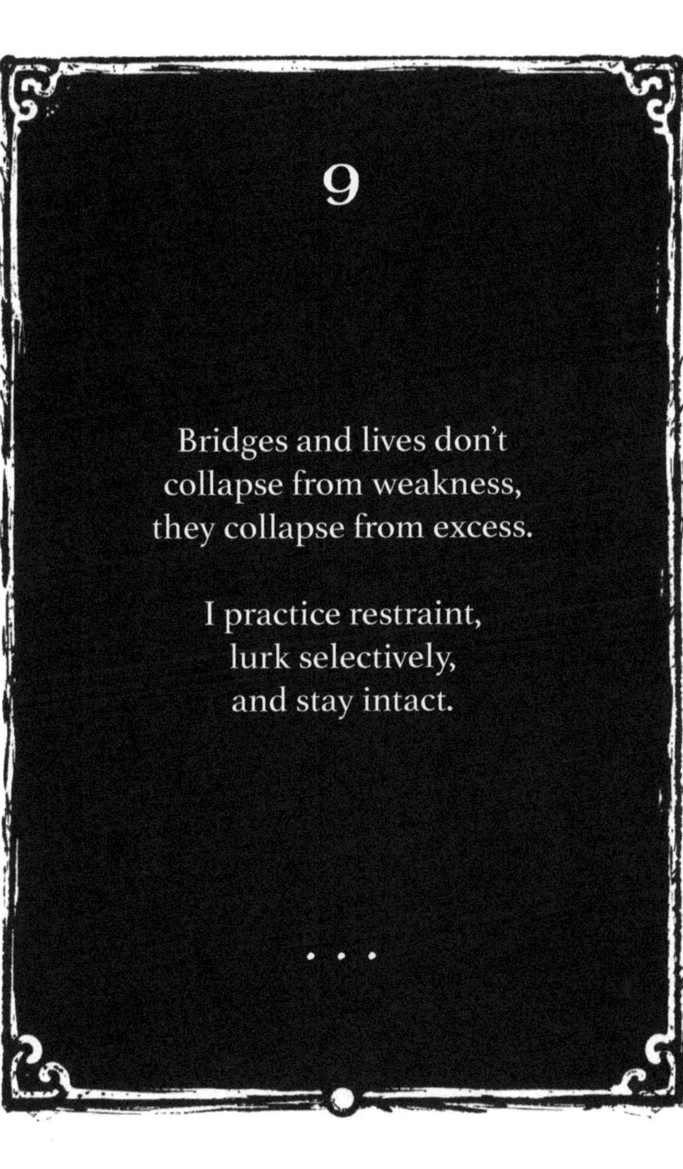

9

Bridges and lives don't
collapse from weakness,
they collapse from excess.

I practice restraint,
lurk selectively,
and stay intact.

. . .

10

Care doesn't require control,
and guidance doesn't need a fist.

I hold the world softly,
like moonlight on my wings,
and nothing breaks.

. . .

MOTHMAN'S
BEST
100% COFFEE

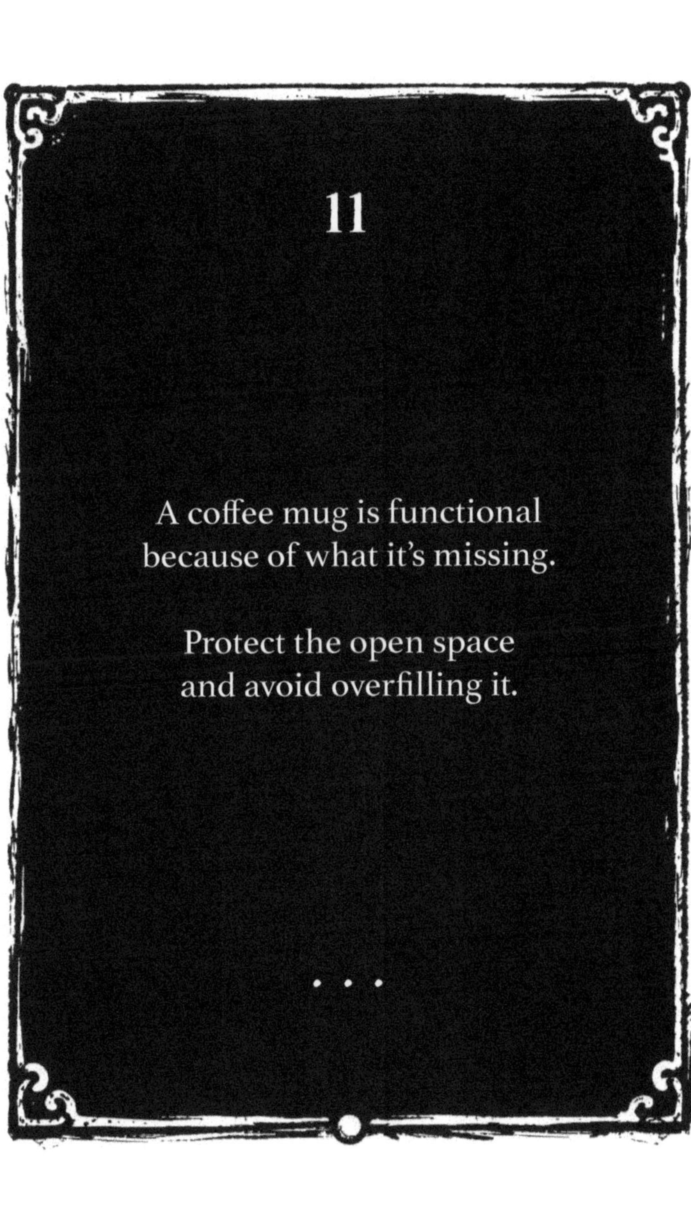

11

A coffee mug is functional
because of what it's missing.

Protect the open space
and avoid overfilling it.

. . .

12

The more you hunt for sparkle,
the more your brain forgets
how to sit still.

I strengthen the core
and ignore the fireworks.

. . .

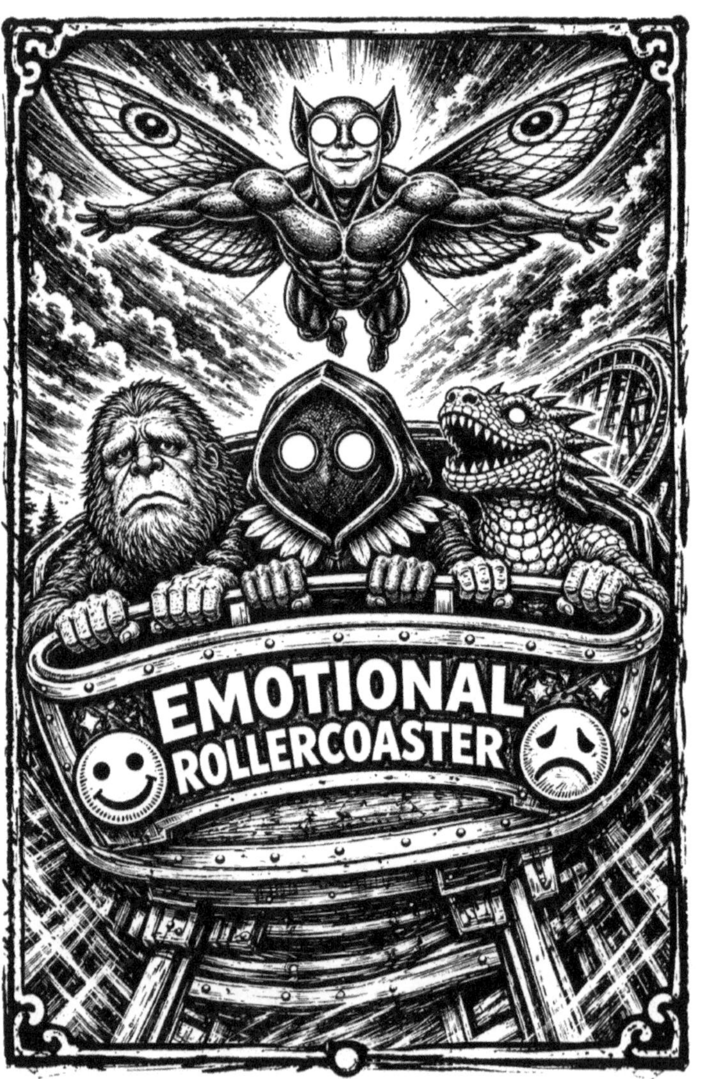
EMOTIONAL
ROLLERCOASTER

13

The thought of applause
can make you anxious
and the thought of disgrace
can make you anxious...
interesting symmetry.

I tend to my not-so-fragile
crypto-mammalian form
and decline purchasing a ticket
for the emotional roller coaster.

• • •

NOPE
NOT HERE

14

The Way refuses to be screenshot,
replayed or pinned down.

I relax into its mystery
and accept that it's been carrying me
the whole time.

. . .

SLOW
DOWN

15

Those who know don't rush,
and those who rush rarely know.

I don't force the moment...
I let it finish unfolding
beneath my feet before I land.

. . .

16

The brain can only panic for so long
before it needs a nap.

I return to the dark,
let stillness do the work,
and watch clarity circle home.

. . .

17

When leadership is quiet,
people feel free instead of handled.

Keep the lights on
without announcing
whose finger flicked the switch.

. . .

18

When harmony fails,
humans start issuing explanations
and policies.

The Way doesn't need a press release
to remain functioning optimally.

. . .

19

I've watched people optimize themselves
into spiraling anxiety.

I do less, mean it more,
and let the knots undo themselves.

. . .

20

The crowd celebrates clarity;
I specialize in dignified confusion.

I drift aimlessly in the dark,
sustained by something vast
that never needed me to understand it.

. . .

21

The Way doesn't advertise
or care what you call it...
it just keeps on shaping everything.

I watch for patterns, not slogans,
and follow the footprints
that it forgets to hide.

. . .

22

What stiffens snaps;
what yields keeps flying.

I stay bendy
and continue lurking like a champ.

. . .

23

Strong winds don't last forever
and neither do blustery opinions.

I speak softly,
stay aligned with what I value
and let the noise get lost in the hum.

. . .

24

If you have to stretch to look tall,
you're already off-balance.

I stand easy, don't wobble,
and let my eyes glow naturally.

. . .

25

The universe didn't wait for
an instruction manual...
it just started universing.

When I feel lost, I breathe
and trust it still knows what it's doing.

. . .

26

Without gravity,
every breeze thinks it's in charge.

I check my center
before blaming the weather.

. . .

27

Forcing clarity is a great way
to invent cracks you'll later pretend
were intentional.

I adjust slowly, stop grabbing,
and let the world finish assembling itself
at its own pace.

. . .

28

Balance isn't something you achieve…
it's something you keep re-adjusting
like a thermostat.

My eyes glow and dim,
but never get stuck on either setting.

. . .

WOULD YOU LIKE
TO INSTALL UPDATES?
COMPLICATE
DISMISS

29

Every time humans treat the world
like a machine that needs to be fixed,
it just breaks differently.

I care for the present and resist the urge
to install unnecessary updates.

. . .

FROM:
TO: WHOM
IT MAY CONCERN

30

Every shove comes
with a return address.

I hover gently
and keep my return address private.

. . .

BE LIKE
WATER

31

Wisdom is knowing
when violence can be avoided,
and feeling its full weight when it cannot.

I follow the Way
that saves smoke for barbecues
and bad decisions.

. . .

32

The Way ran the world just fine
before anyone tried to explain it
or give it a name.

I keep things simple,
know when it's enough,
and let the current handle the rest.

. . .

MOST
POPULAR
CRYPTID

The pursuit of endless victories
is just CrossFit for the ego.

I know my limits,
weather my own storms
and endure like a contender.

. . .

FORTEANBOOK
MOTHMAN
ZERO POSTS

34

The Way is everywhere,
does everything,
and doesn't even need
a social media account.

I lower my ambitions slightly
and somehow seem to achieve more.

· · ·

35

The Way doesn't argue or persuade...
it waits.

I let my eyes glow softly
and trust that those who are ready
will find me.

. . .

EGO
THE
MOTHMAN'S
TAO TE CHING

36

Expansion is often just
pre-collapse enthusiasm.

If you need something to shrink,
just let it keep swelling.

. . .

POTTING
SOIL
FOR INDOOR & OUTDOOR PLANTS
NET CONTENTS 1.5 CU FT (42.5 L)
POTTING
SOIL
FOR INDOOR & OUTDOOR PLANTS
NET CONTENTS 1.5 CU FT (42.5 L)

37

Humans worship extreme effort
like it's proof of value.

I take it easy,
avoid unnecessary interloping,
and watch the world calm itself down
like a toddler cuddling
her favorite blankie.

. . .

38

If your virtue needs a microphone,
it's probably just performing.

I let mine work night shift
without a press release.

. . .

39

Losing your roots
can cause spiritual buffering.

Plant your feet firmly
and let the universe manage
its own settings.

. . .

HOME

40

When I start to drift,
I don't seek bold new horizons…
I adjust my footing.

Most breakthroughs are just
better balance on familiar ground.

. . .

THE
MOTHMAN'S
TAO TE CHING

41

The wise practice, the average dabble,
the foolish laugh... it's biodiversity.

I hover at a sustainable speed
and trust that the ecosystem
will compost the noise.

. . . .

42

Opposition only feels dangerous
until you sit down and
share a cup of coffee with it.

Reality is a group assignment
and no, you can't opt out.

. . .

43

Nothing fits through
what something can't.

I demonstrate
by not demonstrating.

. . .

MOTHMAN
OF THE YEAR

44

I've watched people polish their titles
while their lives quietly fall apart.

I protect what's essential
and refuse to carry anything
that impedes my ability to fly.

. . .

Nothing happening
is usually something happening quietly.

Stop demanding status updates
and let the universe finish in peace.

. . .

46

Unmanaged wanting is why
your soul constantly feels like it needs
another cup of coffee.

The richest creatures I know
aren't hustling...
they're sleeping soundly
through the night.

. . .

47

I learned more hovering quietly
over my favorite bridge
than flying across continents.

The farther you look for answers,
the more they wait patiently at home.

. . .

48

Scholars stockpile trivia...
sages empty their backpacks.

The flight is more enjoyable
when there's less for you to carry.

. . .

49

My eyes don't glow more for believers
or less for skeptics.

I keep showing up
and let consistency handle the logistics.

. . . .

UNKNOWN
$#!TSTORM
IMMINENT!
FREAK OUT
DISMISS

50

Fear sends calendar alerts
for imaginary catastrophes.

I swipe 'dismiss'
and keep my wings steady.

. . .

51

The cosmos raises everything
and still doesn't ask to be tagged.

Meanwhile, humans want applause
for watering a plant.

. . .

52

I once meddled with everything
and wondered why I was miserable.

Now I stay rooted,
refrain from poking the universe,
and sleep like a champ.

. . .

The shiny path looks great
until you realize
it needs constant polishing.

I stick to the plain one...
it holds my weight
and doesn't require
my constant attention.

. . .

54

Ignore the creak and eventually
you'll meet the collapse.

I adjust my wings constantly,
which is why I never crash.

. . .

55

Rigidity rears its ugly head
right before things start to snap.

I stay bendy
and keep my warranty intact.

. . .

BE LIKE
WATER

56

High volume is often just
insecurity using a megaphone.

I use my indoor voice
and let the room lean in.

. . .

57

The more you tighten the net,
the more fish learn parkour.

I give it some slack
and enjoy the natural flow.

. . .

I lurk responsibly
and keep my edges OSHA-compliant.

Real influence
doesn't require a tetanus shot.

. . .

MAIN ST

59

I've seen storms
flatten people who saved kindness
for special occasions.

I practice it consistently
and remain standing alarmingly tall.

. . .

60

I've watched people stir
perfectly good lives into mush.

I cook on low, step away from the stove,
and still manage to eat like a baller.

. . .

61

If you insist on being tallest,
expect strong headwinds.

I stay low enough
to avoid turbulent weather.

. . .

62

Mistakes, bad ideas,
and awkward attempts
all share the same landfill.

I call it compost
and await the
inevitable fruit it will yield.

. . .

63

Most humans reject the dirt path
and build a marble staircase.

Unfortunately,
marble doesn't yield sustenance.

. . .

64

Clay is shapable while it's soft.

Wait too long
and you'll need a chisel.

. . .

65

A room full of experts
can troubleshoot
a problem into existence.

Ease off the intellectual gas pedal
and watch the road
straighten before you.

. . .

66

Mountains pose…
valleys collect rent.

I stay low, avoid the spotlight,
and call it strategic lurking.

. . .

67

Urgency weighs you down.
Ego weighs even more.
Clarity is the blade
that cuts the baggage loose.

I leave the baggage at home
and am able to fly farther.

. . .

CONFLIX
THE
GLOATING
START NEXT EPISODE
SKIP

68

Winning extravagantly
is how conflicts get recurring episodes.

Keep it boring
and let the series get canceled.

. . .

69

Nothing exposes your soft spots
faster than heroic lunging.

I remain cool as a cucumber
and mysteriously hard to dent.

. . . .

70

The Way doesn't clap,
like, or subscribe...
so it struggles with engagement.

I glow softly and let the algorithms
favor louder nonsense.

. . .

THE
SEEKER'S
- GUIDE TO -
ALTERNATE
PHILOSOPHY
AND
BONKERS
OPINIONS

71

Nothing stiffens faster
than a firm opinion.

I stay curious, keep my wings limber
and avoid spiritual arthritis.

. . .

72

Declare yourself untouchable
and watch vulnerability crash the party.

I choose to remain modest
and structurally intact.

. . .

73

Clouds don't hold grudges;
they hold rain.

The Way handles the timing
and doesn't require your approval.

. . .

74

Once you accept that nothing stays,
you stop clutching and start flying.

If you try to conquer fate...
expect some bruising.

. . .

75

When you squeeze people
for every crumb,
don't be surprised
when they look crumbly.

Lighten the load, back up slowly,
and watch their spirit reboot itself.

. . .

76

Anything that brags about being rigid
is already halfway to snapping.

I stay limber, stretch the wings,
and continue lurking
without orthopedic drama.

. . .

The universe trims the loud
and feeds the lean
without announcing quarterly results.

I quit guarding my stash
like a keyed up trash panda
and let the Way rebalance the pantry.

. . .

78

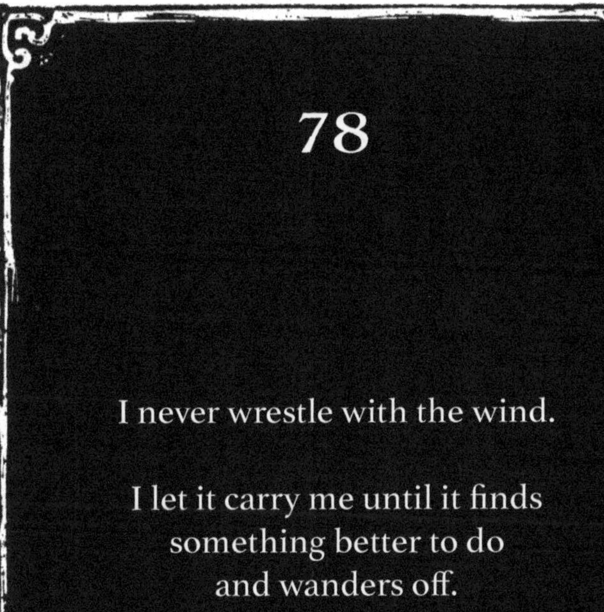

I never wrestle with the wind.

I let it carry me until it finds
something better to do
and wanders off.

. . .

DANGER
HIGH VOLTAGE
KEEP OUT

79

When "sorry" starts invoicing,
the wound keeps renting space.

I evict it quietly
and resume my scheduled lurking.

. . .

80

Bigger, faster, louder
has no idea what "enough" even means.

The Way hits "satisfied,"
logs off, and is in bed by nine.

. . .

81

Do your work with steady hands,
move through the world with mercy,
and refuse to chain yourself
to what you create.

Then step back into
the vast and ancient dark...
the womb of stars
that holds all things without judgment,
without applause,
and without ever asking your name.

. . .

续

ABOUT
MOTHMAN

Mothman is a self-proclaimed renaissance thing.

He's an armchair philosopher, a sculptor, a painter,
a fascinating enigma of which the likes have
never been seen, a gas station coffee sommelier
and a professional lurker.

He loves freaking people out, staring into the void,
giving questionable advice and pulling "silly pranks"
that history often records as "acts of God."

He currently resides everywhere.

He holds a degree in Lurking from
The School of Hard Knocks as well as an honorary
Doctorate of Folklore and Creepy Puppets
from the Banzai Institute.

Mike DiGrazia makes art, writes music
and can, on occasion, string a sentence or two together.
He loves black coffee and speaking in vout.
He currently resides on Earth-o-rooney.

CHECK OUT MIKE'S OTHER STUFF

FINE ART AND BOOKS
instagram.com/digraziart
www.digraziart.com

MOVIE ARTWORK
instagram.com/digmovieart

POZITIVYTRON PROJECT
instagram.com/pozitivytron
www.pozitivytron.com